Candle making guide

Table of Contents

Disclaimer *3*

Introduction *4*

History of candles *5*

Types of candles..*7*

Candles and safety..*9*

Warnings...*11*

Essential items for candle making *12*

Types of wax for candle making:...*13*

Wicks and different types of wicks..*16*

How to make candle – step by step..*18*

Scented candles..*25*

Scented candle – making process.....................................26
Double scented candle – coffee and whipped cream 33

Customized candles..*35*

Something old into something new candle 36
Hand painted candle...43
Dipped, cut and carved candles.......................................49
Candle carving basics...50
Getting started...51
Carving process..53
Customized photo candles 54
Candle inside the candle 56

Disclaimer

Guidelines in this guide are informational only. It is your responsibility to ensure and create accident free environment and supervision when making candles. Everything you do will BE AT YOUR OWN RISK, and therefore we are not responsible for outcome. We do not accept responsibility in respect of any information or advice given in this guide.

Craft process in this guide is presented from personal experience, but we do not imply or guarantee the final outcome. You must accept full responsibility for your actions in candle making process.

Introduction

A candle is a solid wax block, with an embedded wick, which is ignited to provide light and sometimes even heat.

Candles can be made from different types of wax, like bees wax, soy bean wax etc. and can be produced in different colors and different scents.

Candles are quite popular during holidays to highlight that special holiday moments and romantic moments are also unthinkable without them.

You can find candles anywhere from special stores to plain markets, but if you really want amazing candle that will satisfy all senses, than you should create your own.

This guide will teach you how to make simple candles, but also customized ones and even candles from candle leftovers that are quite practical and economical.

History of candles

Candles are for thousands of year's crucial part of human celebrations, but mostly important, they were primary source of light in homes. Still, their origin is not familiar, but is believed and mentioned in historical documents that candles are developed by Ancient Egyptians, but the Romans are generally credited with developing the wicked candle by dipping rolled papyrus (kind of paper) couple times in melted bees wax.

Other numerous evidences are showing us that candles were used not only by these two great cultures, but also many other ones. In Japan candles were made from wax, extracted from tree nuts and early Chinese candles have been molded in paper tubes using rolled rice paper for the wick, and wax from an indigenous insect that was combined with seeds.

These were early stages of candle making and later production was increased. Middle age is credited for usage and rebirth of beeswax. Animal fat was replaced very quickly with beeswax, because it burned pure, without smoke and smoky flame. These types of candles were used in church ceremonies but also in homes of wealthy individuals. Thanks to them, candles have become extremely popular on courts, where thousands of candles were used to illuminate royalty events and celebrations. Soon, everybody wanted to enjoy in flickering candle light.

Colonial time brought us the first type of scented candles and colonial women brought this invention. Still, extracting wax from the bayberries was extremely long and boring, so these candles were soon expelled from use.

18th century was characterized by whaling industry, so logically whale oil was next candidate to produce candles from. This type of candle, made from whale fat, had quite unpleasant smell, but it could stay firm even during summer months. Wax derivate from whale oil was named spermaceti (by whale name) and it was in use until paraffin was discovered. Paraffin wax was introduced in the 1850s, after chemists and scientist discovered how to separate waxy substance in petroleum and refine it. Paraffin wax was instantly popular because it burned clear and without any unpleasant smell. Again after all these invention and discoveries, appearance of light bulb in 1879 meant end of candle era.

When it comes to another essential part of a candle, braided wicks were also invented in 19th century. Earlier wicks were in form of twisted cotton threads that actually burned very poor and needed constant maintenance.

Today candles have gained their popularity again and all have moved couple steps forward from their initial use. Candles now symbolize celebrations, mark romance, love and intimacy and give a warm and interesting welcome to any home. Beside this they also accent home decors in unique way.

Types of candles

Candles can be found in various sizes, shapes and scents. Of course they all have their precise name, in order to distinguish them. Here are most popular types of candles and their characteristics:

Pillar – this is a type of free-standing candle, usually with 3-inch diameter and sometimes even more. They can also have one or more wicks all depending on their size. Pillar candles can stand on their own, but they should have some kind of protection during burn, so heat-proof candle holder would be ideal. This type of candles is great to use as decoration and they will blend perfectly in any interior, regardless are they burning or not.

Taper – this is a type of slim/slender candle that needs to be placed in candle holder. It is ideal for dinner events so it is sometimes known as dinner candle. Taper candle is quite thin but also very high, from 6 to 18 inches. You can find them in variety of colors, to suit any occasion and mood.

Container or jar candle – as you can see, this type of candle is poured into jar or similar heat-proof container. It comes in variety of colors and scents.

Gel candle – is perhaps one of most interesting candles, because it is usually decorated with different wax beads, sometimes dried flowers and even sand. Gel candles are produced from gelled mineral oils, or gelled synthetic hydrocarbons. There are two types of gel candles, soft and hard. Soft gel candles are poured in containers, to maintain candle shape, while hard gel candles have bigger consistency so they are suitable for free-standing candles. They burn and act like any other candle, so if you were skeptic about these small works of art, give them a chance. You will be very pleasantly surprised.

Tea light candles – those small candles poured in metal container are known as tea light candles. They are usually in cylindrical shape and about 1-1 ½ inch high, sometimes plain and sometimes scented and colored.

Votive candles – are small cylindrical candles, usually 1 ½ - inch in diameter and around 2-2 ½ - inches high. They are designed to easily be placed in a cup or votive holder. Votive candles were very popular for religious ceremonies, and therefore did not had any color or scent. Today things are different and can be found in numerous colors and scents.

Floating candles – are designed to float on water and therefore they have low, stable profile. Of course, since they are so attractive and interesting, manufactures have produced them in different type of shapes, from simple smooth to realistic ones.

Specialty candles – are perhaps most realistic type of candles. They can be found in any 3D shape imaginable, from animal, floral to special like Santa or Halloween pumpkins. This type of candle can be molded or sculptured by hand and are mostly used for decorative purposes.

Candles and safety

Candles can now be bought anywhere, but if you want candle, with your own personal signature, here is a simple way how to do it. Of course we will start with plain candle. When you get the basics, it is easy to change them and customize however you like.

Before we start with candle making process, you should know some basic kit you must own and safety manners.

Candle making safety

Safety is No.1 and therefore you should always be careful and protect yourself from heat and melted wax. Burns caused with melted wax or paraffin can be extremely painful and dangerous. When melting a wax you should use double boiler method. It is not quite fastest method to melt paraffin, but is certainly the safest. Wax can sometimes burst into flames without any warning signs.

There are three primary safety concerns in candle making:

- Wax safety – be careful to avoid burns and protect yourself from heat
- Fragrances – handle carefully, because during vaporization some fragrances might be toxic if inhaled
- Spills and wax drops – spilled wax can really mess up with your carpet and kitchen surfaces.

So, before you start to make candles, prepare your working surface and all essential candle making items, like wax, scissors, wick, paraffin, thermometer and boiler. You can cover your working space with some newspapers or old table cloth. Your working surface needs to be organized to ease entire candle making process, so organize all necessary items.

Just like with any other job or home-made making, you should do it slowly and methodically. This way results will be great and you will have just what you imagined. Follow candle making rules strictly, especially if you are beginner. Later, when you ear technique you can play and be creative and do whatever you want.

Warnings

Essential oil warning:

Scented candles are unthinkable without essential oils, but they can be very tricky. These oils are highly concentrate and they can eat through plastic and cause some serious skin irritations, so measure and pour them carefully. If your skin gets in direct contact with essential oil, rinse it immediately under cold water and wipe your hands after well.

Melting wax warning:

Like mentioned earlier, wax can bur if reaches certain temperature, so never leave your wax unattended. You should treat wax with certain dose of respect and be aware of its power. Wax will burn at 180°and it will not worn you with boiling bubbles that is hot. It will just start to smoke and eventually burn. If you want to avoid these troubles, melt wax/paraffin in double boiler. Sill if you want to melt wax directly over heat source, do not leave room and DO NOT LEAVI IT UNATTENDED.

Additional warning is to keep wax away from open flame, because many accidents may happened. You should use thermometer to always know precise temperature of your melted wax in order to avoid overheating and potential burning.

By following these crucial rules, you will enjoy in your candle making process and in final product.

Essential items for candle making

Double boiler is must have in candle making. If you want to avoid all unnecessary troubles, like wax burning, than double boiler is the key. Choose whatever you like, and the best are simple circular boilers, that can easily fit in each other.

Next thing you will need, especially if you are beginner is quality thermometer. Once you learn how to make candles and remember appearance of melted paraffin/wax, than you could try without thermometer, but for beginners, stick to it. You can find different types of thermometers and even simple cooking ones are good for this purpose.

Another important thing is pour pot. This is actually pot from which you will pour melted wax/paraffin into molds. Pour pots should be made from aluminum, but a glass Pyrex measuring cup will also do the trick.

When you have necessary pots and boilers, next thing is to choose ideal type of candle wax. There are different types of them, and here are their characteristics, so you can easily choose ideal for you.

Types of wax for candle making:

Paraffin wax:

This is perhaps most popular and world known type of wax to make candles. It comes in unscented, white and tasteless form, with melting point from 110-150°F. Higher temperature will make it burn. Paraffin wax is a by-product of raw oil refinement process. It comes in white color or even colorless.

What candles can be produced?

You can use this type of wax for any type of candles, and melting point will determine what candles to make out of it.

- Low melt point paraffin is used for container or jar candles. This type of paraffin has less than 130° melting point.
- Medium melt point paraffin is used for candles that can stand on their own, like pillars, votive etc. It has malting point around 130-150°F.
- High melt point paraffin wax is used to produce candle shells, like hurricane candle shell or for over-dipping. Melting point is over 150°F.

As you can tell this type of wax comes in versatile forms and that is perhaps the reason why is so popular and why does it have wide range of use.

Soy wax:

Soy wax is relatively new type of wax, developed in the early 1990s as "green and natural" alternative to petroleum-derived paraffin, and the natural but expensive bees wax. Just like paraffin wax, soy wax comes in different melting points and therefore you can produce different types of candles from soy wax, still most popular use of soy wax is for container or jar candles.

Soy wax comes in form of flakes, which makes it ideal to scoop and measure. Soy wax can be easily combined with other types of wax, like paraffin or beeswax and even oils, like palm oil. If you want candle that is declared as soy wax candle, than it should at least contain 51% of soy wax.

Beeswax:

Beeswax is considered as original candle wax and it is one amongst the oldest types of wax that is used for candles. Beeswax comes from the bees and they use it to construct honey comb, in which they preserve their honey.

You can produce any type of candles with this type of wax. It is quite useful to make instant candles, by just rolling beeswax sheet with some wick in the middle. Beeswax is heavy, sticky wax and it is used for, like mentioned, for different types of candles, like votive, pillars, container candles and even molded creations.

You can found beeswax in form of blocks, small pellets that melt quite easily and in form of sheets, ideal for instant candles.

Gel wax:

Gel wax is actually mineral oil that has been thickened with a special polymer into a clear, slow burning wax.

There are three types of gel wax:

- CLP grade – Low density: it melts and pours the easiest, but is not quite thick to support embeds and it can hold only up to 3% of fragranced oil. This gel is good for low scented gel wax candles without embeds.

- CMP grade – Medium density: this type of gel wax will hold up to about 5% fragrance oil and quite well all embeds, especially if you are using small shell, glitter etc. Since it has medium density it melts and pours relatively easy.
- CHP grade – High density: this type gives you the ability to suspend dense pigments, glitter or other embeds. High density gel wax is slightly harder to melt and pour, but thanks to that density it keeps up to 6% of fragrance oil.

Gel wax unlike traditional wax, melts in much higher temperatures, between 180°-200°F, so you need to heat it directly over heat source and not in double boiler.

Thanks to higher density gel wax, manufactures have now chance to create pillar candles and not just container candles like they could only do in the past.

Palm wax:

Palm wax is quite similar to soy wax, only it is not made from soybean oil, but from palm oil. Palm wax is very firm, brittle wax that works very well in pillars and votive,

Special characteristic of palm wax is that it produces a crystalline or feathered effect on candles that is quite attractive and interesting. You can combine it with soy wax to make it even more harder, but to keep that special effect that only palm wax can produce.

Wicks and different types of wicks

Most consumer think that candles shape, color or scent are crucial elements of candle. However experienced manufacturers will say that wick is the essential element of quality candle. The purpose of wick is to deliver wax to the flame. Wicks actually draw melted wax into flame to burn.

All wicks are made of bundle of fibers that are braided, twisted or knitted together. These fibers absorb the liquefied wax and carry it to the flame by capillary action.

Most quality wicks are made from braided, knitted or plaited fibers, to encourage slow and consistent burn. Twisted wicks are of lower quality than knitted or braided wicks. They burn much faster because of their construction that allows more fuel (wax) to quickly reach the flame.

In general there are three major categories of wicks, used in candle making – core, flat and square/round wicks.

Cored wicks

Cored wicks have a rigid core, made of paper, zinc or cotton. This core keeps the wick standing up straight even in a melted container of wax, like in container or votive candles.

Metal cored wicks usually contain zinc or tin core and they are perfectly safe when it comes to health. Cored wicks are usually braided or knitted.

Flat wicks

These flat-knitted or plaited wicks are usually made from three bundles of fiber. They are very consistent in their burning and curl in the flame for a self-trimming effect. They are most commonly used types of wicks and come in sizes that indicate the number of piles or strands in the wick for example; 24 ply, 30 ply, etc.

Flat and square braid wicks tend to curl into flame, making them to burn cleaner.

Square and round wicks

These knitted or braided wicks also curl in the flame, but are more robust and round than flat wicks. Squared wicks are preferred for beeswax applications, but also for other candle applications like pillars and tapers and can help inhibit clogging of the wick that may occur with certain types of waxes, pigments or fragrances. Rounded wicks are ideal choice if you are making palm wax or soy wax candles because they will allow for thicker wax to flow better through the wick.

How to make candle – step by step

If you are big fun of candles and you want to make some of your own, here is simple and easy method how to do it.

In these couple easy steps you will learn how to make plain candle, that you can later customize and when you learn the basics you can later play with colors and scents.

You will need:

- Wax – paraffin wax beads
- Wick
- Container or a mold
- A double boiler with spatula to stir
- Skewer and paper clip – to secure the wick
- Scissors – to trim the wick
- Fragrance – additional

Step 1. Gathering all essential items

Before you start with candle making it is the best to place together all necessary items. This way entire candle making process will be much easier.

Step 2. Melting the paraffin wax

Melted paraffin

As explained earlier wax has its burning point and it will really burn. To avoid accidents like that to happen, use double boiler as shown on picture. This way you will safely melt paraffin wax. You can also place thermometer in, so you can precisely know temperature of wax. You can also add 5% of beeswax into paraffin wax to get cleaner burn.

Procedure: Place paraffin wax (with 5% of beeswax additionally) in double boiler. Heat until wax is transparent and runny or until it reaches 130°-150°F – depending on type of wax you are using.

When wax is melted pour it in pouring pot, aluminum or Pyrex measuring glass. This way you can easily pour melted wax in any type of mold or container.

Step 3. Preparing the candle wick

Prepared and centered wick

Wick is essential part of all good and quality candles. Good wick choice is 50% of successfully created candle. Another important thing when it comes to wicks is to center them properly in container or mold. There are different ways and we bring you one quite simple:

Process: Place paper clip on one end of candle wick and tie another end of wick on skewer. Paper clip will pull down candle wick and make it straight, while skewer will secure wick of dropping in the candle wax. When you finish this step, you are ready to pour melted wax in container or mold.

NOTE: When you pour liquid wax into container or mold, sometimes bubbles may appear. If this happens, pierce them with toothpick or needle.

Step 4. Almost done and ready to burn

Ready to burn

Process: When you pour paraffin wax into container or a mold, let it rest for a day. This way you will get really nice candle, with firm paraffin that will burn really nice and clean.

Scented candles

Scented candles are special kind of candles. We love them because they illuminate our space but also surround us with a pleasant smell. This type of candles if perhaps the most popular type and therefore we dedicate this entire chapter just to its majesty, the scented candle.

When we take a look back in the history, we cannot go without one question; when did the scented candles first appear? By just looking in historical facts, we can conclude that first scented candles are bayberry candles, made in colonial time by American women's. This was the first natural scented candle, but because making process was long and bit boring, these candles were expelled from manufacturing and use.

Essential oils have been around for thousands of years, but when people realized that thy can combine it with the wax, era of scented candles has begun. We do not know accurate date, but thanks to essential oils and discovery that they can combine with other materials, like wax, brought us lovely home decorations that simply lure us with amazing scent.

Another merit of essential oils is now possibility to mix and combine them in order to get more interesting and double or triple scented candles.

Since scented candles are such nice touch and are great for relaxing moments, here are simple instructions how to make your own.

Scented candle – making process

There are many different ways to make scented candle. We bring you the easiest one, but the key to great scented candle is quality wax and essential oil. Poorly made scented candle will have pleasant smell when not burning, but when burned it will start to spread unpleasant smell. This can be very frustrating, but if you follow next instructions, everything will be just great.

Scented holiday candle

You will need:

- Old cups – some old with flowers would be great
- Scissors – to trim candle wick
- Wicks with metal wick holders
- Scented oil – since this is holiday candle opt for almond and orange scents
- Thermometer and double boiler
- Bamboo skewers
- ½ pound paraffin wax

Step 1. Preparing the wax

Preparing the wax

Process: For this candle us wax with melting point around 140°F. Melt wax in double boiler, because it is the safest way. You can use thermometer to precisely know the temperature.

Step 2. Adding the scented oil

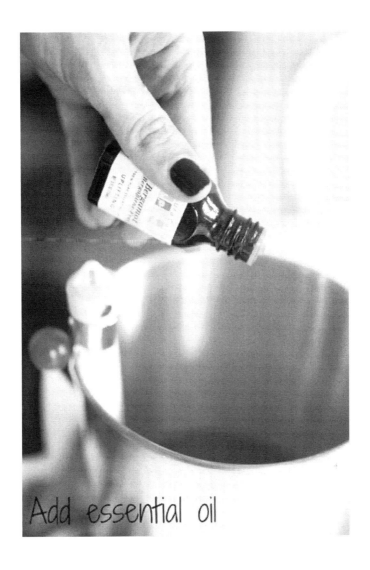

Add essential oil

Process: Add couple drops of essential oil in melted paraffin wax. You can add 2-3 drops or more if you want intensive scent. Stir with spatula.

NOTE: You can additionally add some color.

Step 3. Pouring wax into cups and adding candle wicks

Place candle wick

Process: Pour melted scanted wax into candles and wait for one minute. Carefully insert wicks and secure them with skewers (like shown in previous example). If some bubbles appear pierce them with toothpick or a needle. Pour on top some wax additionally, until you have nice, smooth surface.

Step 5. Lightning it up

Process: Let your candle "dry" and firm up for a day. It is ready to be lighten up and you can enjoy in your homemade holiday candle.

Double scented candle – coffee and whipped cream

Double scented candles are absolutely amazing, because they provide you with double scent by your choice. There are different double scented candles that you can buy, but sometimes combination of double scents are not adequate to us, so here is simple way on how to make double scented candles, with scented by your choice.

Ingredients:

- 1 pound paraffin or beeswax - melting point around 140°-150°F
- Container or a mold
- Braided candle wick
- Scissors – to trim the candle wick
- Skewers – to center the wick
- Fragranced oil No. 1 – like coffee scent
- Fragranced oil No. 2 – like whipped cream
- Some whole coffee beads
- Double boiler and thermometer

Candle making process:

Step 1. Bring some water to boil in the bottom of a double boiler.

Step 2. Add ½ pound paraffin wax in double boiler. Heat and follow temperature with thermometer.

Step 3. When wax is melted add 3 drops of coffee fragrance oil. Stir well. Meanwhile add coffee beads in container or a mold. Center the candle wick and secure with skewer.

Step 4. Pour coffee scented wax over coffee beads and let it cool for two hours.

Step 5. Bring some water to boil in the bottom of a double boiler.

Step 6. Melt rest of paraffin wax and add whipped cream fragrance oil, 4 drops.

Step 7. Pour whipped cream scented wax over coffee scented wax. Pierce bubbles if they appear and let it cool for half an hour.

Step 8. Additionally decorate with some candle shreds and let candle sit overnight.

Step 9. In the morning remove from the mold (if you used one) and your double scented candle is ready to burn.

NOTE: To avoid bubbles poke wax 2-3 times around wick. This will prevent air pockets, from building up in the wax.

Customized candles

Customized candles are candles with your own personal touch. You can make them in different colors, with different scents and decorate with lace, beads, dried flowers etc.

In this chapter we will bring you interesting ideas how to make customized candles, on easy and simple way.

Customized candles can be ideal as a gift or you can make some of your own for different holidays, like Christmas, New Year and spooky for Halloween.

There are different types of customized candles from simple one, decorated with decoupage technique, medium hard to make with candle paint directly applied to candle or difficult to make using carving technique.

Once you get the basics and you let your creativity lose you will be able to produce awesome-looking candles.

Something old into something new candle

Something old into something new is type of candle made from old candle leftovers. It would be such a shame and waste of course to throw and not re-use those candle pieces. You can melt them and make perfectly great candle. Of course you cannot re-melt them over and over, but one re-melting is just fine. This way you can save up some money and still have wonderful candle and if you add some lace as decorative element, result will be amazing.

You will need:

- Candle leftovers
- Some new candle wick
- Glass container
- Lace ribbon and some decorative pearl beads
- Burlap ribbon
- Wood glue
- Scissors and skewers
- Hot glue gun
- Some candle dye and fragrance oil

Process:

Step 1. Prepare all necessary items and protect working surface with old newspapers.

Step 2. Cut old candles into similar cubes, so they melt evenly.

Chop the candles

Step 3. Melt candle pieces in double boiler, using thermometer to know exact temperature. Add candle dye and few drops of fragrance oil.

Step 4. Center candle wick in candle glass container. Pour in melted candle wax into candle container. Secure candle wick with the skewer.

Melt the wax and pour into glass container

Step 5. Let candle cool for three hours before decorating.

Step 6. Decorating: Apply thin layer of wood glue onto candle glass container and let it dry for a minute. Apply over burlap ribbon and press firmly so it glues.

Apply wood glue onto glass container

Step 7. Apply some hot glue onto burlap and glue some lace over it. You can decorate additionally with some pearl beads or even tie around thin sateen ribbon.

Apply burlap onto glass container

Step 8. Left candle overnight before you light it up.

Apply lace with glue gun and enjoy in candles

Hand painted candle

Hans painted candles will take out all your creativity and this is unique way to show your inner artistic side. There are two easy ways to apply paint, directly by hand or by using patterns.

You will need

- Pillar candle. preferably white
- Candle liner in different colors
- Some patterns and toothpicks

Process:

Step 1. Prepare all essential items and cover working surface with newspapers.

Step 2. Place prepared pattern onto candle and directly apply candle dye on. Spread it over pattern, using palette knife.

Apply color over pattern and
spread it using palette knife

Step 3. Remove pattern after 20 seconds. You must do it very carefully, because dye can smudge.

Step 4. When you decorate one side of the candle, you can also decorate another one. You do not have to use patterns. Instead some candle lining colors and toothpicks will be just enough. So, apply directly some candle dye onto candle.

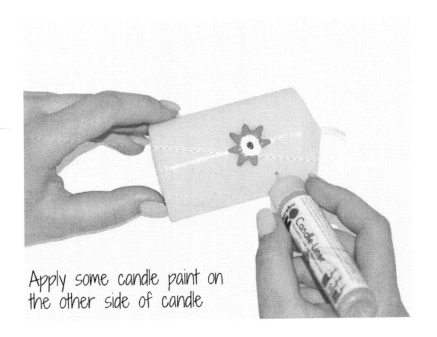

Apply some candle paint on the other side of candle

Step 5. Using toothpicks spread some coloring to make unusual and interesting shapes. This is part of the process where you can play and let your creativity to be absolutely free.

Apply some more dye and make patterns using toothpick

Step 6. Let the candle aside at least for two hours, it's then ready to be used.

NOTE: You can sprinkle some glitters over fresh candle paint to make the candle even more interesting.

Dipped, cut and carved candles

When you get all the basics about the candles and when you feel that you are ready for the next step, you can play with the wax in numerous ways. You can carve it, dip in colored wax and make all kind of carves for more interesting candles.

For these candles you will need a lot of practice to get the wanted results, but you will see in the end that all effort pays off.

Dipping technique can be used as another decorative technique. It is quite easy to perform and with this technique you can make another type of colored candles. You just need to dip your candle into dissolved colored wax, let it dry and remove after wax drips with a knife. This way you can only color half of the candle, while other half can remain un-colored.

Carved candles are unique and are definitely queen among the rest of the candles. There are different types of them, all depending from manufacturers crafting abilities; greater abilities greater candle.

Most important thing in entire candle process is wax. For carved candles you will need wax with medium melting point, around 130 degrees. Paraffin wax is therefore ideal for this kind of job, but you can try with some other types of wax.

Candle carving basics

Before you start with the carving, as essential item you will need the candle. Pillar candles are ideal for this type of job, because they have necessary structure that can be carved.

Carved candles are actually candles with core made from plain candle, but these types of candles are dipped repeatedly in colored wax in order to get nice thick layer that can be carved.

You can dip candle core in two colors (colored wax) but if you want you can dip it in even more colored wax, to create multi colored layers that will give you more interesting carves.

Candle should be at the end thicker for about 1 inch and this is thickens that is satisfying.

When you finish with dipping the candle you will have around 7 minutes to finish all carving process. After that wax will become too firm and it will eventually break.

When it comes to cores you can use pillar candles as a core, but if you want greater candle opt for core in shape of 6 sided star.

When it comes to carving you can look for inspiration at the beginning in some books or guides, but later you will be only limited with your imagination.

Getting started
You will need:

- Candle core – simple pillar candle with longer candle wick
- Wax
- Candle dye – two or more colors, white color is must
- S shaped hook
- Double boiler and scissors
- Container with lukewarm water

Step 1. Before candle making you should protect your working surface with the old newspapers.

Step 2.Bring all essential items on working surface.

Step 3. Place candle wax in double boiler. Decide how many colors you want. You will need a container of white wax, and container of cleared wax for each candle you make, in addition to one container for each additional color that you want.

Step 4. Add the candle dye to each container. Still leave one with cleared wax to add that extra gloss to the candle. Amount of candle dye will effect on final candle color.

Step 5. Tie candle wick around S shaped hook, firmly and dip the candle in white wax. This way you will have great base for coloring. Leave it for 30 seconds.

Step 6. Take out the candle and dip it in water for 3 seconds. Take out the candle and wipe the water drops with the hand.

Step 7. Dip the candle in colored wax, for example red color, and let it in for 3o seconds. Take it out and repeat Step 6.

Step 8. Dip the red colored candle again in the red colored wax. This way you will have nice intensive color.

Step 9. Repeat Step 6 and dip the candle into colored wax, for example yellow color. Dip the candle twice, like explained in Step 8. You can repeat this as many times as you want or as many colors you desire.

Step 10. When you finish with the candle dipping as final step, dip the candle in clear melted wax in order to get nice glossy surface.

Step 11. Hang the candle when you are done with the dipping. Remove wax drips with a craft knife. You will have 7 minutes before wax is too firm to be carved.

Carving process

You will need:

- J-shaped or circular blade

Step 1. Start carving at the top of candle and pull the blade downward, almost to the bottom. Cut into your candles up to ½ inch or ¼ inch.

Step 2. Twist the cut wax into spirals. Press back the wax into groove you cut. Repeat the carving and twist the four times around the candle in even increments.

Step 3. Carve the wax in varying lengths at the different levels around the rest of candle. This way you will get interesting design. Bend the small cuts down and under and press the base to the candle.

Step 4. Set candle aside for four hours or overnight before burning.

Customized photo candles

This type of candles is basically made with famous decoupage technique. This technique is art form entails pasting cut-outs, usually paper, to an object, in this case candle, with several coats of lacquer or in this case wax.

Certain picture (photo, or some other) is applied on candle and pasted to a candle with simple heating of candle. When candle heats for example with hair drier, 1 mm of candle is starting to melt, allowing you to paste a photo or some other decoration. This technique is simple and you can do amazing decorations with it.

Another way of applying decorations or making decoupage is with hot glue gun. With hot glue gun you can make 3D applications quite easily, for example flower; you can paste several layers of flower onto candle and you will have nice 3D effect.

Once you get the basics you can make more interesting candles with different pictures and applications.

For customized photo candle you will need:

- Candle – pillar or votive
- Vellum paper
- Waxed paper
- Hair drier

Process:

Step 1. Print a copy of your favorite picture on vellum paper.

Step 2. Cut out the picture and place it on the candle, making sure it fits.

Step 3. Wrap the waxed paper around the candle and photo, carefully making sure that waxed side is of the paper is facing the photo.

Step 4. Heat the photo through waxed paper, using hair drier, for 15-20 seconds.

Step 5. Peel the wax paper gently and make sure that the picture is anchored to the candle. If not repeat Step 4 again, until picture is nicely set.

Step 6. This is additional step and you can decorate your candle with ribbons etc.

Candle inside the candle

This type of candle combines two types of candles, or two types of wax, gel wax and paraffin wax. It basically represents votive candle wrapped in gel wax. With burn of just one wick, all waxes are melting and it burns just like regular candle, but the look is amazing.

You will need:

- Thin dinner candle
- Fragrance – that is hydrocarbon compatible and non-polar
- Candle dye
- Medium density or high density gel wax
- Glass container and double boiler
- Some melted paraffin wax – or few drops of melted wax from burning candle

Process:

Step 1. Heat double boiler and place in gel wax. Follow temperature with thermometer. Gel wax needs more time to melt than paraffin wax.

Step 2. Add candle dye or even food colors, few drops of fragrance by your choice and stir well to combine.

Step 3. Add few drops of melted wax to the bottom of glass container. Place on the thin dinner candle and press until it is stick to the bottom.

Step 4. Pour over melted gel wax, carefully, so you do not cover the candle wick.

Step 5. Left candle overnight before burning.

NOTE: Size of candle dictates the size of glass container. For thinner candles choose more narrow containers.

NOTE: Before combining gel wax with fragrance oil, make test with small quantities to see are they compatible.

Finished product

Printed in Great Britain
by Amazon.co.uk, Ltd.,
Marston Gate.